JESUS TAUGHT IN PARABLES

Three Bible Stories for Children

Children's Jesus Books

ONE TRUE FAITH
RELIGION & SPIRITUALITY

First Edition, 2020

Published in the United States by Speedy Publishing LLC, 40 E Main Street, Newark, Delaware 19711 USA.

© 2020 One True Faith Books, an imprint of Speedy Publishing LLC

All rights reserved.

Without limiting the rights under the copyright reserved above, no part of this publication may be reproduced, stored in or introduced into a retrieval system, or transmitted, in any form, or by any means (electronic, mechanical, photocopying, recording, or otherwise), without the prior written permission of the copyright owner.

All images in this book have been reproduced with the knowledge and prior consent of the artists concerned, and no responsibility is accepted by producer, publisher, or printer for any infringement of copyright or otherwise arising from the contents of this publication.

One True Faith Books are available at special discounts when purchased in bulk for industrial and sales-promotional use. For details contact our Special Sales Team at Speedy Publishing LLC, 40 E Main Street, Newark, Delaware 19711 USA. Telephone (888) 248-4521 Fax: (210) 519-4043.

10 9 8 7 6 * 5 4 3 2 1

Print Edition: 9781541977501
Digital Edition: 9781541977518
Hardcover Edition: 9781541977525

See the world in pictures. Build your knowledge in style.
www.speedypublishing.com

TABLE OF CONTENTS

THE PARABLE OF THE GOOD SAMARITAN 5

THE PARABLE OF THE SOWER 27

THE PARABLE OF THE MUSTARD SEED 51

INTRODUCTION

The parable of the Good Samaritan is found in the Gospel of St. Luke Chapter 10, verses 25 through 37. Jesus told this parable after he was asked a question by a well-known lawyer and scribe. This scribe who was well versed in the Law of Moses and the Old Testament; asked Jesus "What should I do in order to have eternal life?". Jesus answered the question by telling this parable.

THE PARABLE

Once upon a time there was a man who decided that he wanted to go on a journey. The man was in a city called Jerusalem. The place that he wanted to go to was Jericho. The day finally came when he set out on the journey and he was all by himself.

A MAN GOING ON A JOURNEY FROM JERUSALEM TO JERICHO.

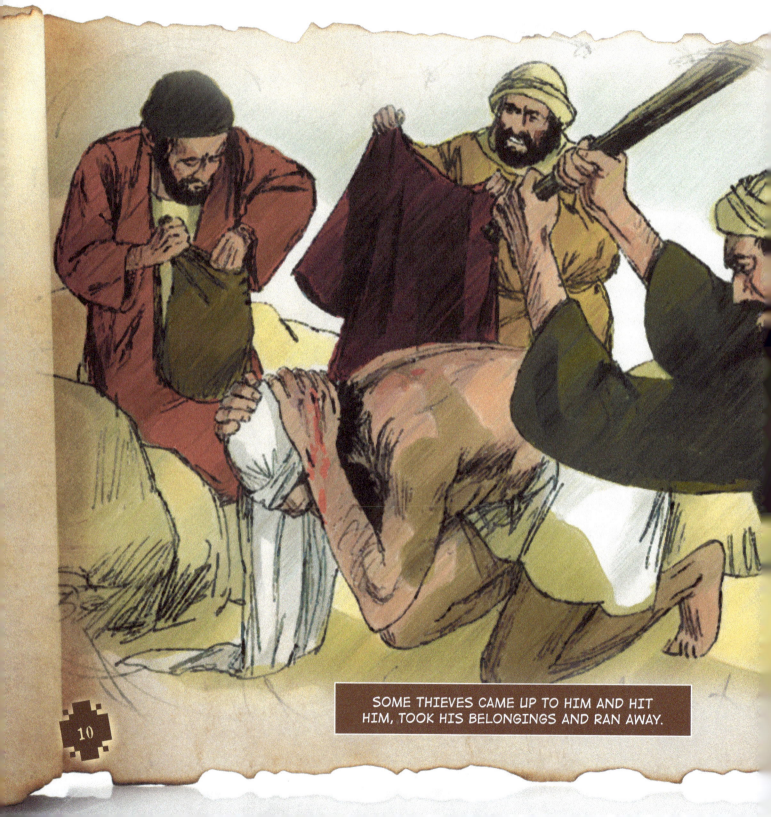

After he was travelling for a while, some thieves came up to him. They hit him, took his belongings, even his clothes, and ran away. The injured man was left all by himself on the side of the road. He was hurt so badly that he was almost dead!

After a while, a man happened to walk down the same road. This man was a priest (a leader of a religion). When the priest saw the badly beaten man, he did not rush to help him. Instead, he went to the other side of the road and kept on walking.

Not too long after that, another man happened to walk down the same road. This man was a Levite (a man whose ancestors were from Hebrew priests from the tribe of Levi). He, too, caught a glimpse of the poor man who had been beaten by thieves. Just like the priest, as soon as the Levite saw the injured man, he ignored him.

Finally, a third man came along. He was a Samaritan (a man from Samaria). As he got nearer and noticed the terrible state that the beaten man was in, he immediately felt sorry for him.

He quickly went over to the man and started to take care of him. The Samaritan bandaged up the poor man's wounds. Then, he took some oil and wine that he had with him and placed it in the cuts to help them heal.

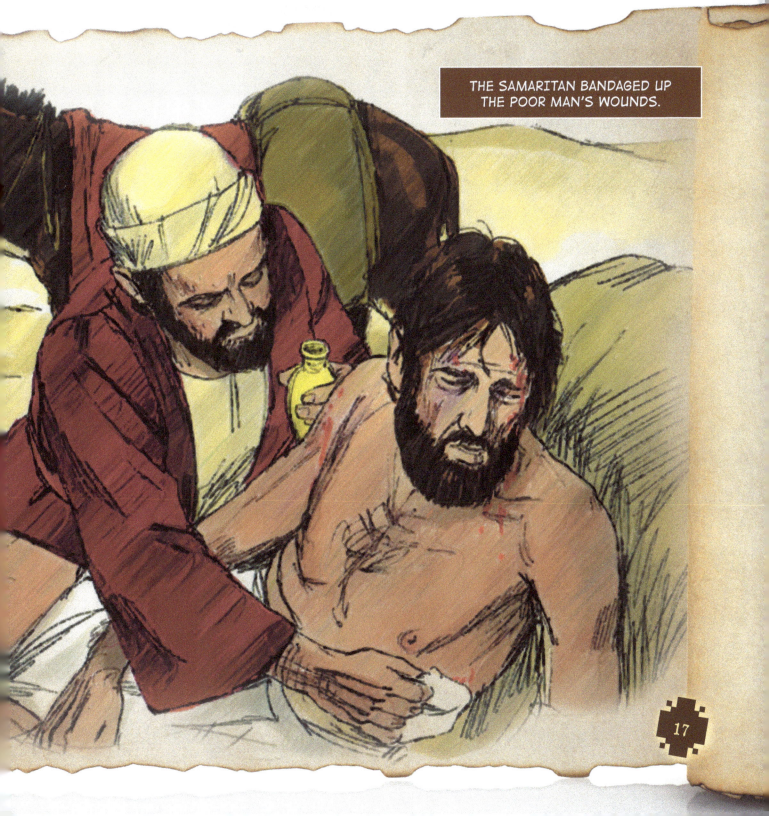

Finally, he lifted the man up and put him on his own donkey. The Samaritan then walked along side the wounded man on the donkey until they reached an inn. The Samaritan took the man with him into the inn.

The Samaritan could only stay at the inn for one night. However, before he left, he took some of his own money and gave it to the innkeeper. The Samaritan said that the money, which was around two pence, was to be used to help the man who had been hurt. The Samaritan then said that if more money is needed to be spent to help the man get better, that he, the Samaritan would pay it when he came back.

THE SAMARITAN PAID THE INNKEEPER TO TAKE CARE OF THE MAN WHILE HE WAS GONE.

JESUS TOLD THE LAWYER TO SHOW COMPASSION AND HELP THOSE IN NEED.

Jesus then asked the lawyer a question. He wanted to know that out of the three people who had come across the injured man, who the lawyer thought was the neighbour. The lawyer replied that it was the man who had compassion on the injured man and helped him. Jesus told the lawyer to do the same thing.

COMPREHENSION QUESTIONS

1. Who asked Jesus a question?
2. Why was the question asked?
3. Why did Jesus tell the parable?
4. In what city did the man start his journey?
5. Where was the man headed?
6. Who attacked the man?
7. Who was the first person to discover the man hurt and lying on the road?

8. Did he help the injured man?

9. Who was the second person to discover the man hurt and lying on the road?

10. Did he help the injured man?

11. Who was the third person to discover the man hurt and lying on the road?

12. Did he help the injured man?

13. Who did Jesus say was the neighbour of the injured man?

14. True or False? Jesus told the lawyer to help someone who has been hurt.

LESSON OF THE PARABLE

We all need to be compassionate and kind to others. It does not matter who that person is. When someone has a need and we can help, we should do so. We should help them as much as we can and not expect anything in return.

THE PARABLE OF THE SOWER

INTRODUCTION

The parable of the sower is found in St. Matthew 13;1-23, St. Mark 4:1-20 and St. Luke 8:4-15. It was told to a large crowd of people who had come to listen to Jesus. It was near a lake. Because so many people had come, Jesus got into a boat and told the parable while the people stood on the shore. He told many parables that day and he started with the Parable of the Sower.

THE PARABLE

There was once a farmer who went to sow (plant) some seeds. He sowed the seeds in different places. One of the places where the seed was being scattered was along a certain path. When the seeds landed, some birds came along and gobbled them up.

Some of the seeds fell on areas of land that contained a lot of rocks instead of much soil. In this area, the seeds were able to spring up very fast because the soil was not too deep. However, the sun soon scorched the plants because they did not have strong roots. Before too long, they withered away.

SOME OF THE SEEDS FELL ON AREAS OF LAND WITH A LOT OF ROCKS.

Some of the seeds fell in places that had a lot of thorns. Unfortunately, the plants got choked when the thorns grew up.

SOME OF THE SEEDS FELL IN PLACES THAT HAD A LOT OF THORNS.

SOME SEEDS FELL ON SOIL THAT WAS VERY GOOD.

Some seeds managed to fall on soil that was very good. When this happened, the farmer was able to reap a good crop. It was so good that it produced a crop that was way more than the seeds that had been planted.

Jesus then told the people that those who had ears should hear. After Jesus said this, His disciples came up to Him and asked why he told parables to the people. Jesus said it was because the people did not know the secrets of the kingdom of heaven. It was the disciples who knew these secrets.

JESUS SAID THAT THE DISCIPLES KNOW THE SECRETS OF THE KINGDOM OF HEAVEN.

Jesus taught in parables because some people do not see things even though they're looking; and they do not understand the message even though they hear.

Jesus then told the disciples that those who have been given things will receive more and they will have a lot. Those who have not received, will have the little bit that they already have, taken from them. Jesus then explained this is the reason He teaches in parables. Even though people are looking, they do not see things and even though they hear, they do not understand the message.

Jesus spoke about the prophecy that the Prophet Isaiah made about people always listening to something and seeing it, but never being able to understand it. The reason is that some people's hearts have become hard. They do not hear much with their ears and they have shut their eyes. If they used their eyes to actually see, their ears to actually hear and their hearts to understand and turn, then Jesus would heal them.

Then Jesus told His disciples that they were blessed because they can see with their eyes and hear with their ears. Some righteous (good) people and even a lot of prophets had longed to see what the disciples had seen and to hear what the disciples had heard but they did not.

After that, Jesus told them to listen to the meaning of the parable of the sower, which is this:

When a person hears the message about the kingdom of heaven but is not able to understand it, what is sown in the person's heart is snatched away by the evil one. The seed that was sown along the path represents (shows) this kind of person.

THE SEED THAT WAS SOWN ALONG THE PATH REPRESENTS PEOPLE WHO HEARS THE MESSAGE BUT IS NOT ABLE TO UNDERSTAND IT.

The seed that ended up on the ground that had rocks represents people who are filled with joy when they hear the message. However, they do not last very long because they have no root. When trouble or hard things happen, they immediately fall away.

THE SEED THAT ENDED UP ON THE GROUND THAT HAD ROCKS REPRESENTS THOSE THAT HEAR THE MESSAGE BUT DO NOT ACT ON IT.

The seed that fell in the thorns represents people who hear the message but they become too focused on life's worries. They allow riches to deceive them and they do not become fruitful.

> THE SEED THAT FELL IN THE THORNS REPRESENTS PEOPLE WHO HEAR THE MESSAGE BUT THEY BECOME TOO FOCUSED ON LIFE'S WORRIES.

However, the seed that found good soil represents someone who understands the message once it is heard. This person is the faithful one who gets a lot of crop, so much more than what was sown in the first place.

> THE SEED THAT FOUND GOOD SOIL REPRESENTS THOSE WHO UNDERSTAND THE MESSAGE AND SHARE IT TO OTHERS.

COMPREHENSION QUESTIONS

1. In how many Gospels is this parable told?
2. Where was Jesus sitting when He told this parable?
3. Where were the people when Jesus told the parable?
4. Who sowed the seed?
5. On what type of ground did the first seed fall?
6. On what type of ground did the second seed fall?
7. On what type of ground did the third seed fall?
8. On what type of ground did the fourth seed fall?

9. Who asked Jesus why he chose to tell parables?

10. Why did Jesus say He chose to teach things in parables?

11. What kind of person did the seed that fell along the path represent?

12. What kind of person did the seed that fell along rocks represent?

13. What kind of person did the seed that fell in thorns represent?

14. What kind of person did the seed that fell on good soil represent?

LESSON OF THE PARABLE

Jesus told this parable to show that different people will respond different ways to the Gospel or good news of Jesus Christ. Jesus, Himself, is the sower and the seed is God's word.

Moreover, the parable shows us how the condition of our hearts is very important to how we will decide to respond to the Gospel of Jesus Christ. Our decision is shown by our actions after we have heard the message.

THE PARABLE OF THE MUSTARD SEED

JESUS TELLS THE PARABLE OF THE MUSTARD SEED.

INTRODUCTION

Three of the Gospels of the New Testament record the parable of the mustard seed. It is found in the Gospel of St. Matthew Chapter 13, verses 31 through to 32; in the Gospel of St. Mark Chapter 4, verses 30 through to 32 and the Gospel of St. Luke Chapter 13 verses 18 through to 19.

THE PARABLE

Jesus told the people that the kingdom of heaven can be compared to one grain of mustard seed. He told them that a mustard seed is very tiny.

A MUSTARD SEED IS VERY TINY.

A MAN PLANTING A TINY SEED IN THE GROUND.

One day, a man took one of these tiny mustard seeds and he planted it in the ground.

After a while, the seed started to grow. From that one tiny seed, a great tree grew. It was the greatest tree of all. It grew to be so big that birds would fly to it and rest on its branches.

COMPREHENSION QUESTIONS

1. What did Jesus compare to a mustard seed?

2. True or False? A mustard seed is tiny.

3. Who planted the mustard seed?

4. What happened to the mustard seed?

5. What did the birds do?

LESSON OF THE PARABLE

The parable is to show the Kingdom of heaven. The mustard seed stands for the Church or followers of the Gospel message of Jesus Christ. The message of the Gospel of Jesus Christ and the early Church would start with humble beginnings and in one area. However, it would become powerful and spread all over the world.

The good news of Jesus would bring joy and rest to those who accepted it. This is represented by the birds coming to rest on the branches of the mustard tree.

Visit

www.speedypublishing.com

To view and download free content on your favorite subject and browse our catalog of new and exciting books for readers of all ages.

CPSIA information can be obtained
at www.ICGtesting.com
Printed in the USA
BVHW062101280121
599006BV00005B/272